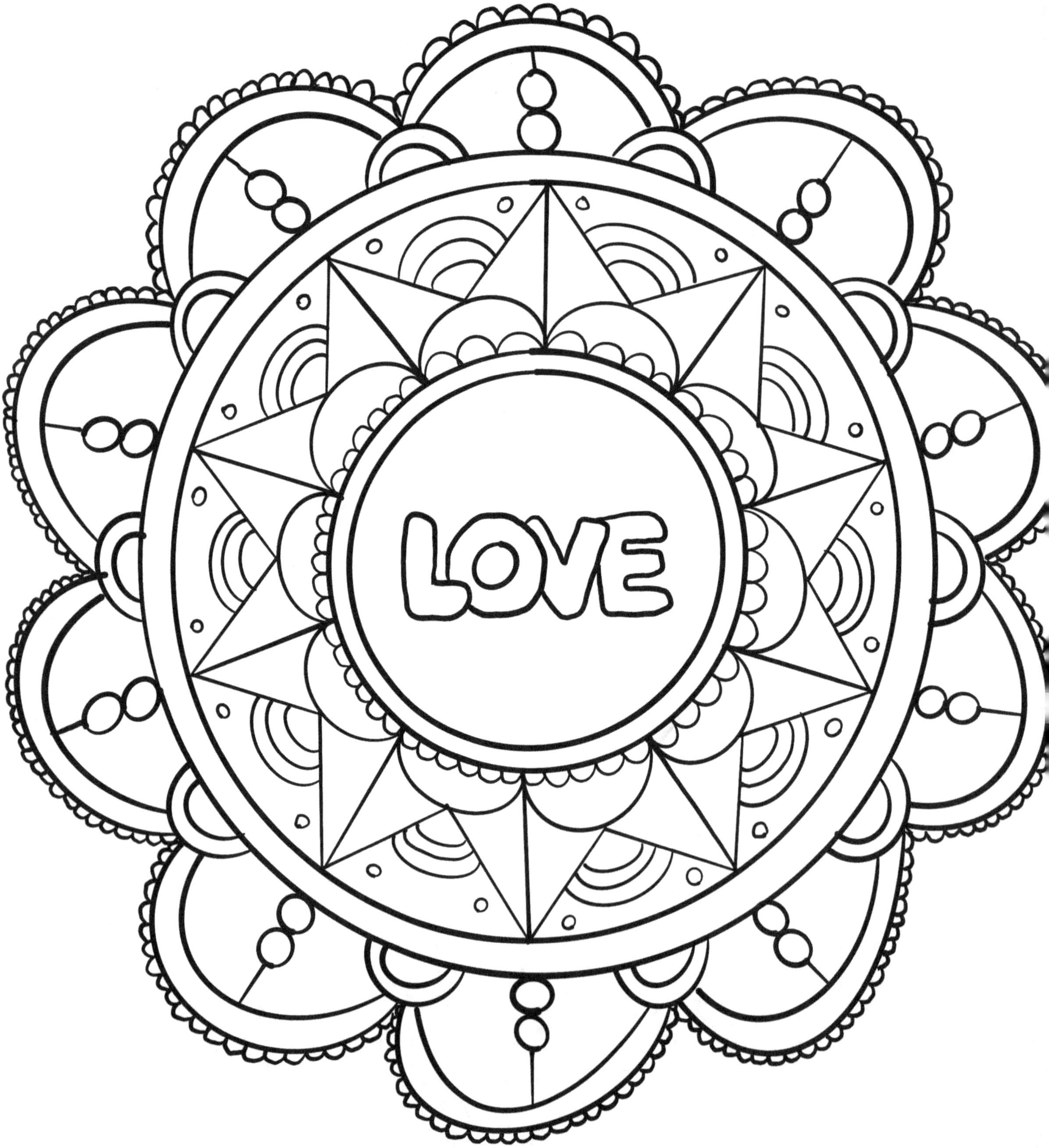
LOVE

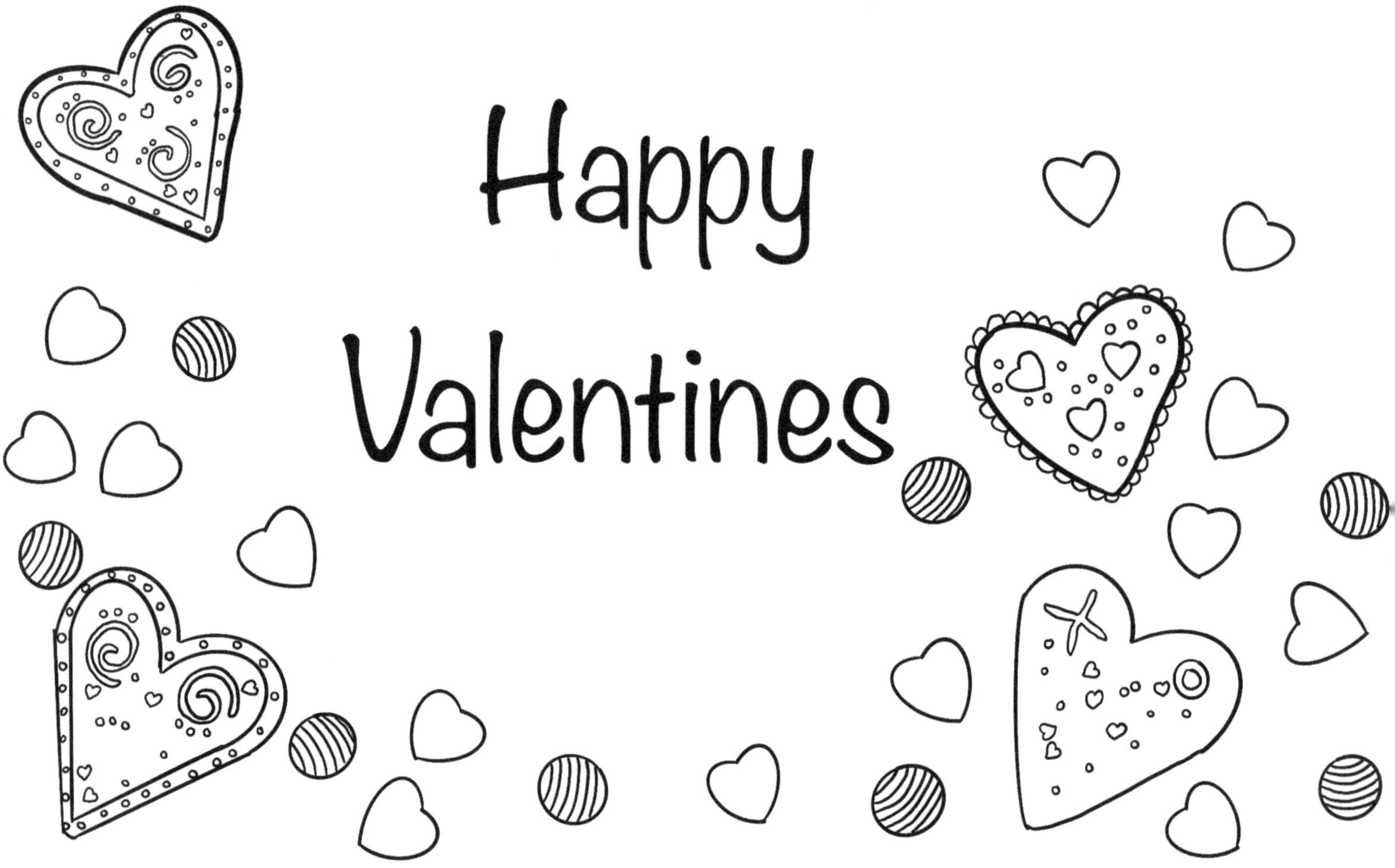
Happy
Valentines

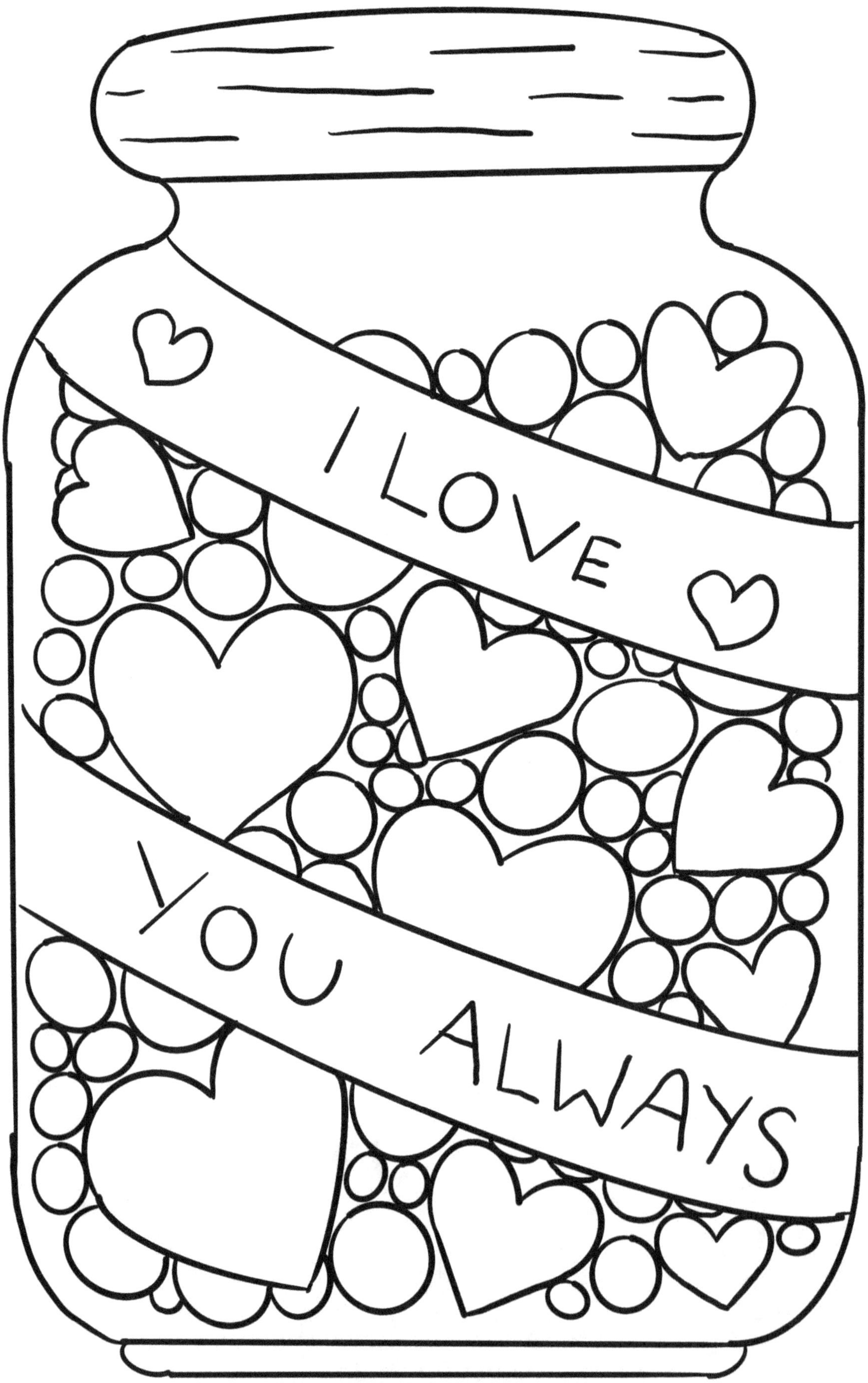
I LOVE
YOU ALWAYS

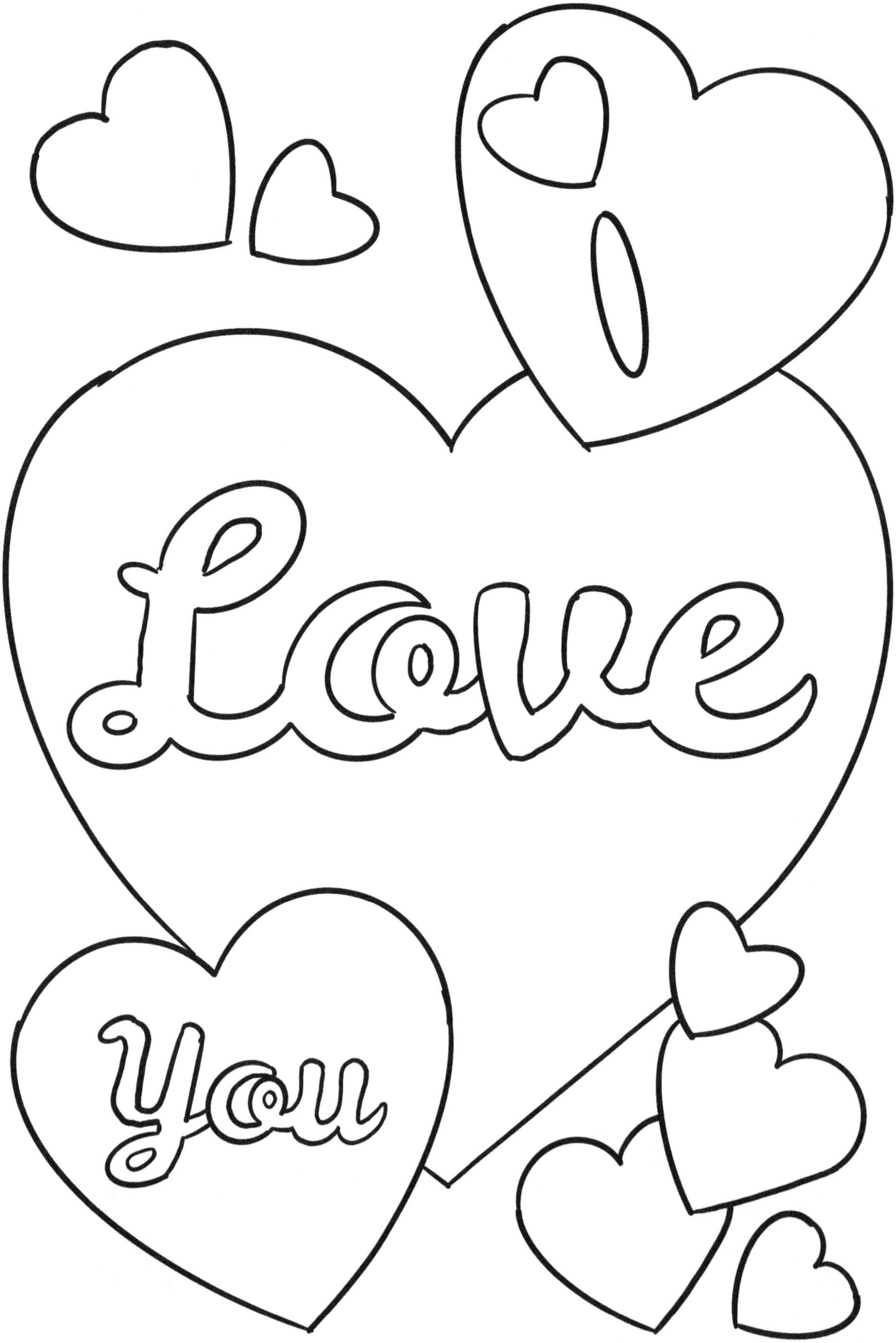
I
Love
You

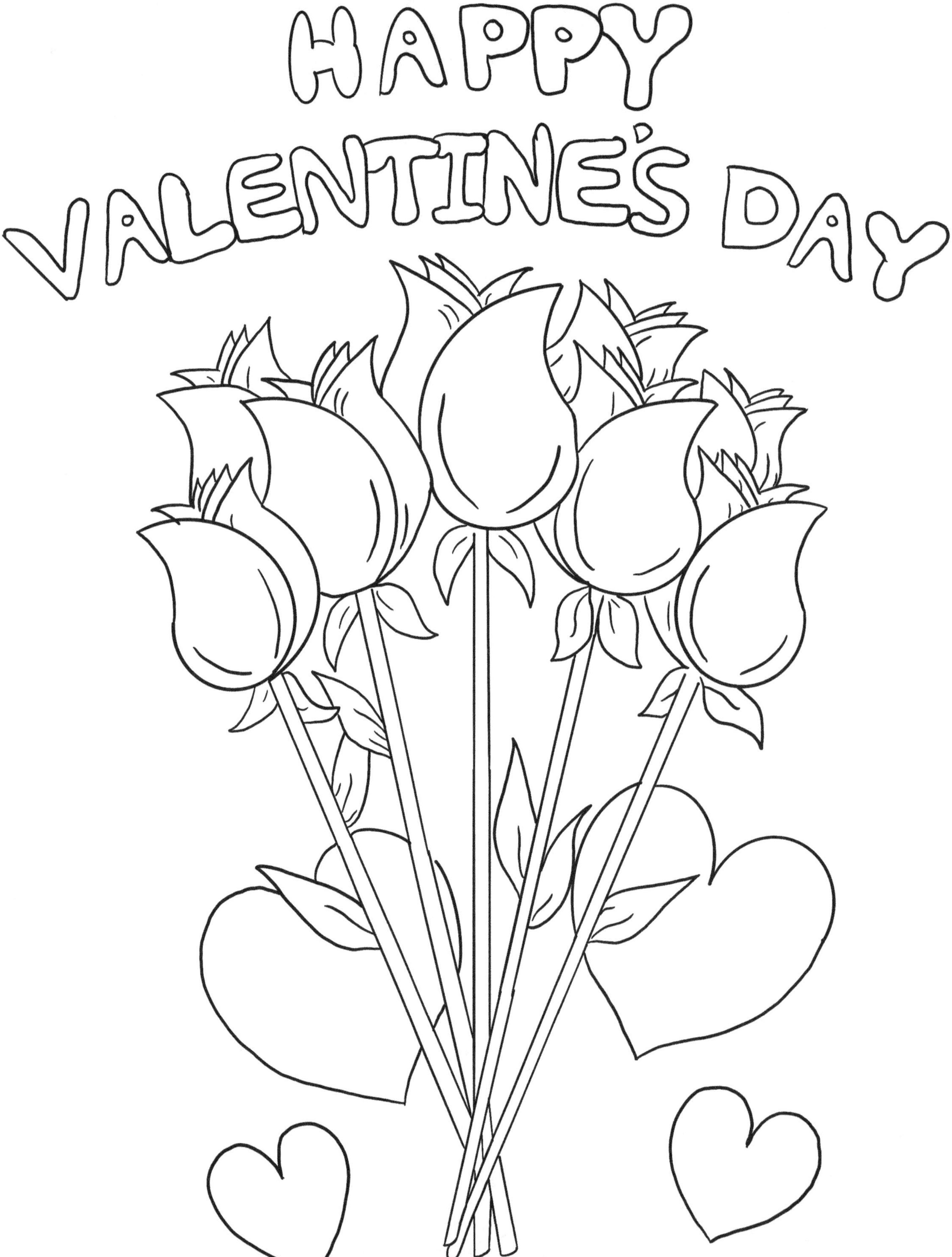
HAPPY
VALENTINE'S DAY

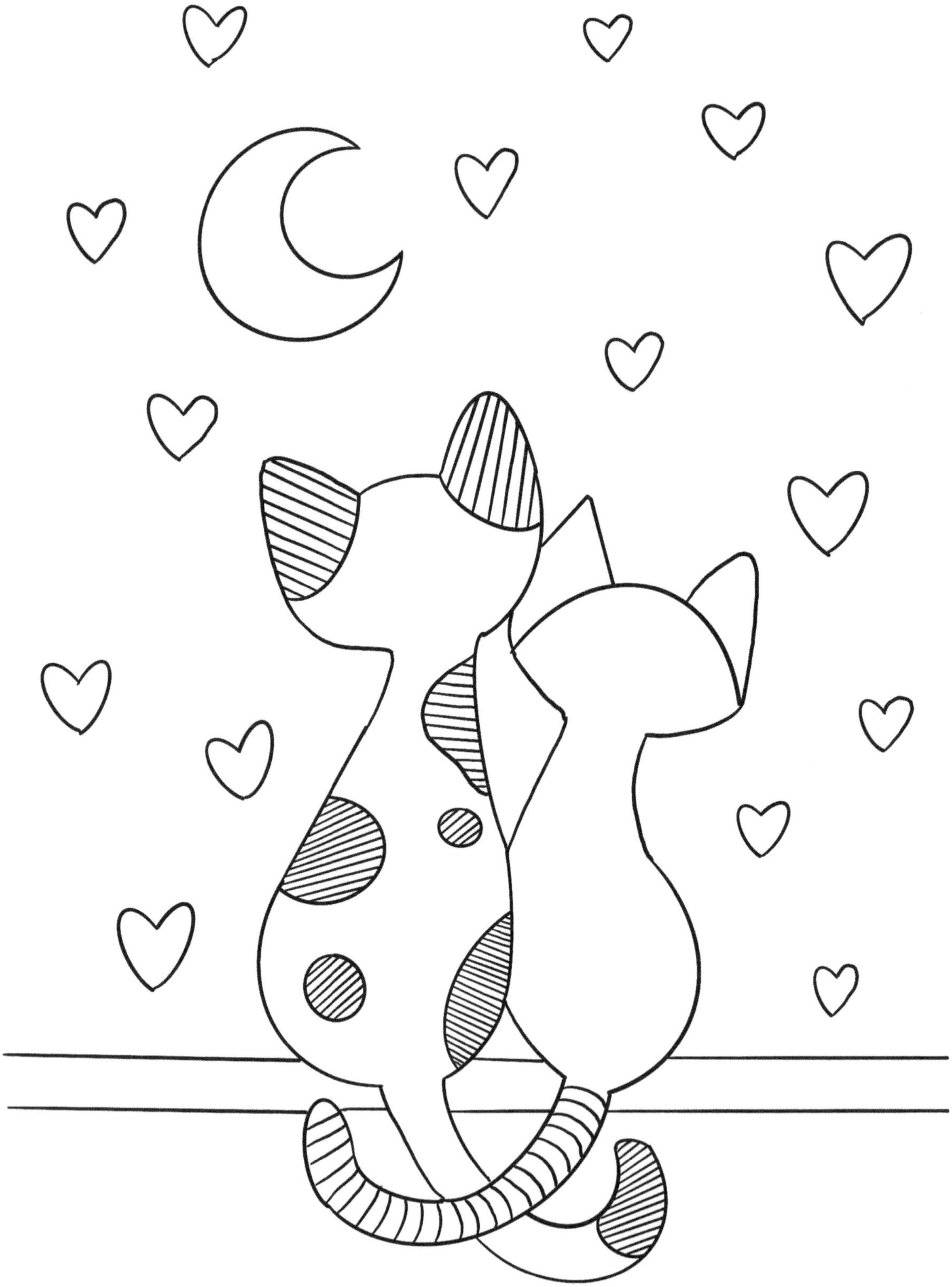

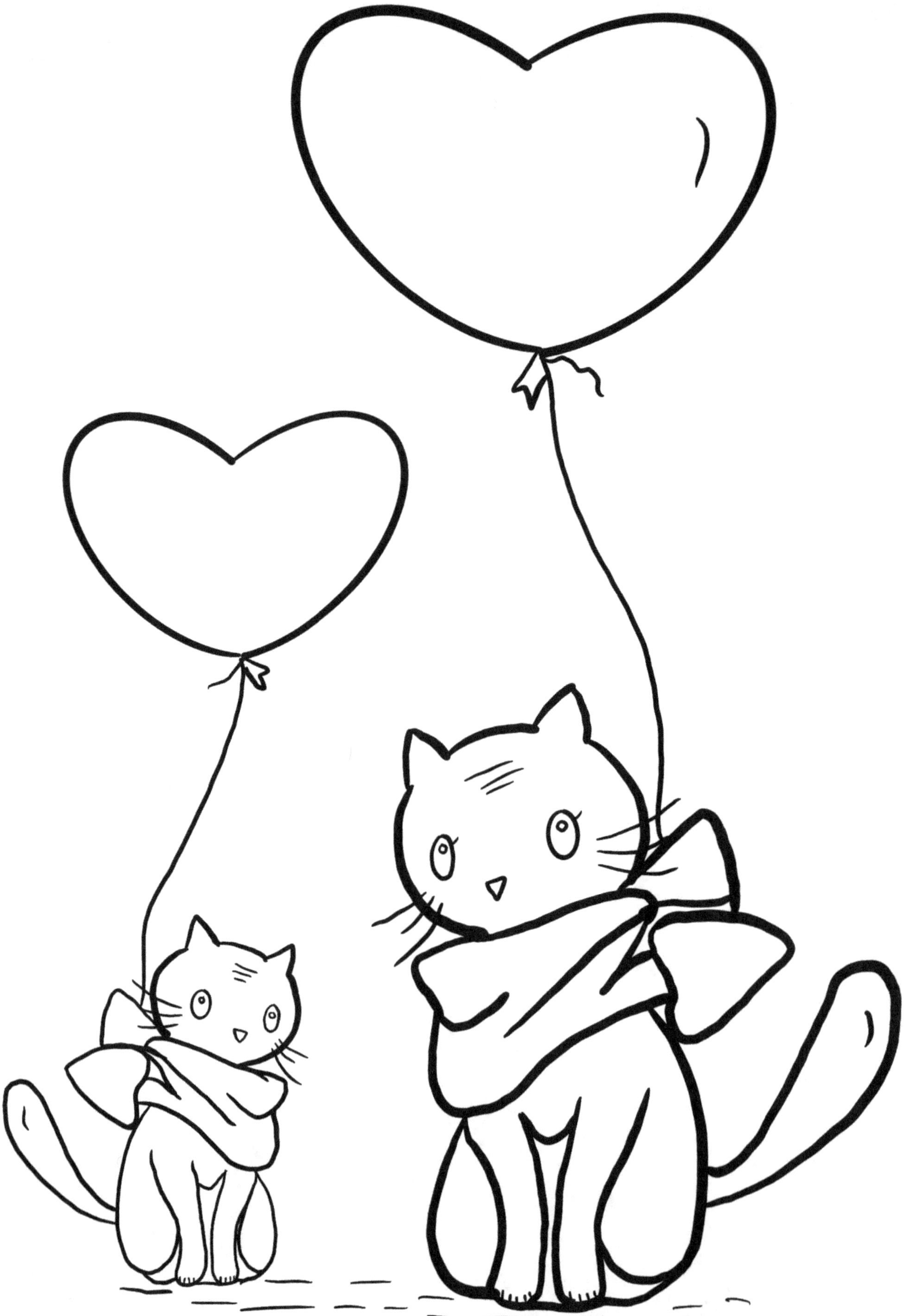

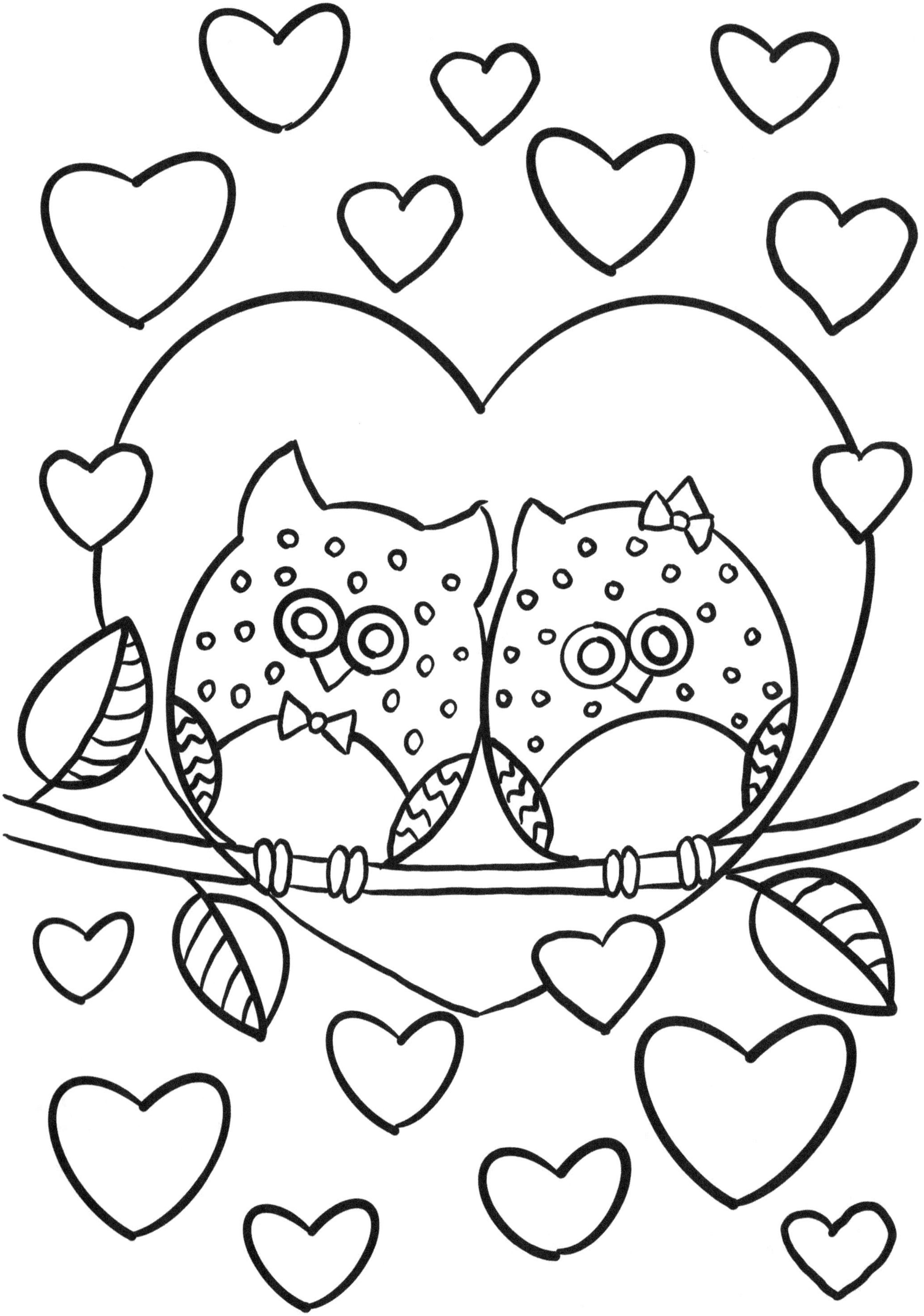

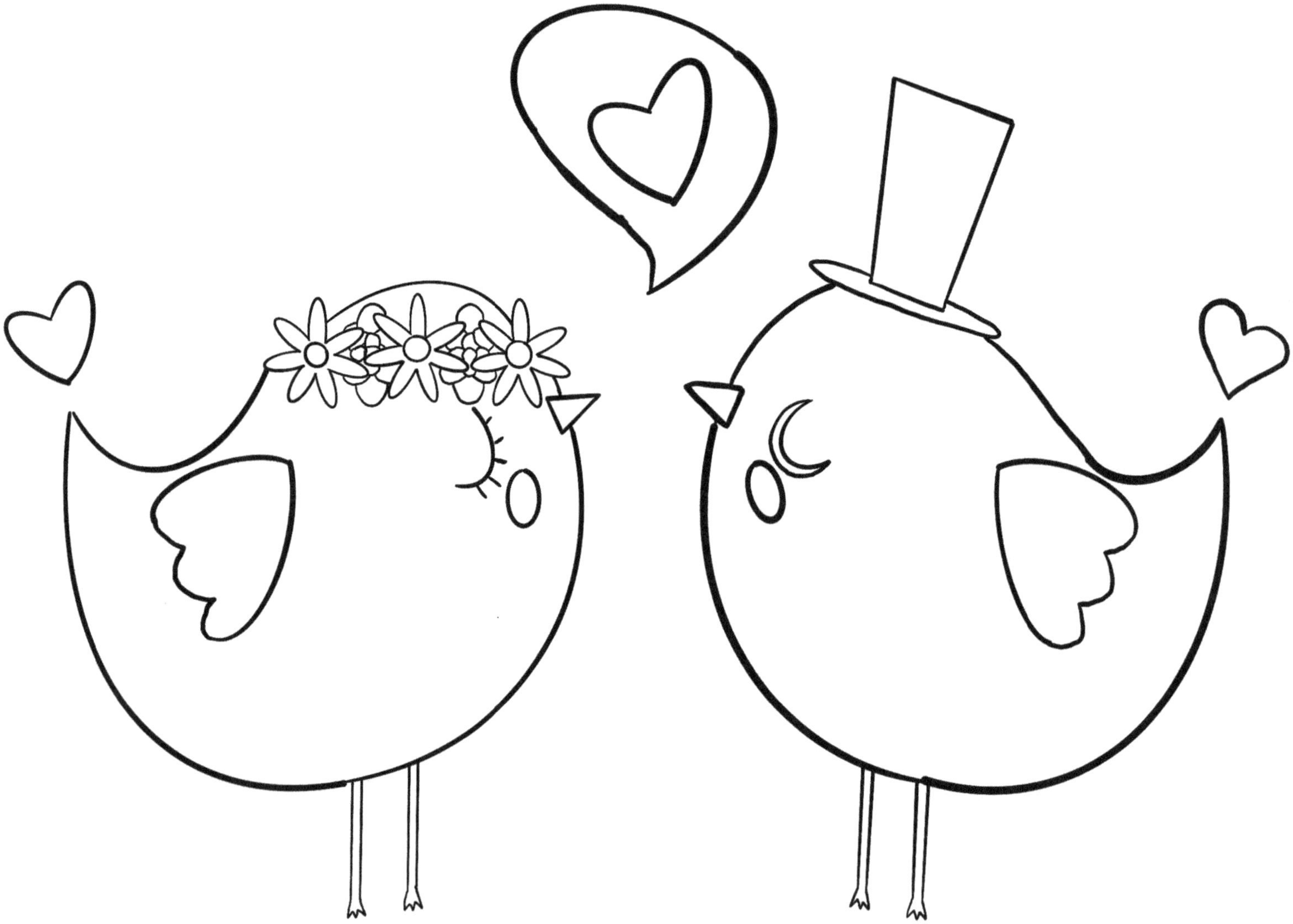

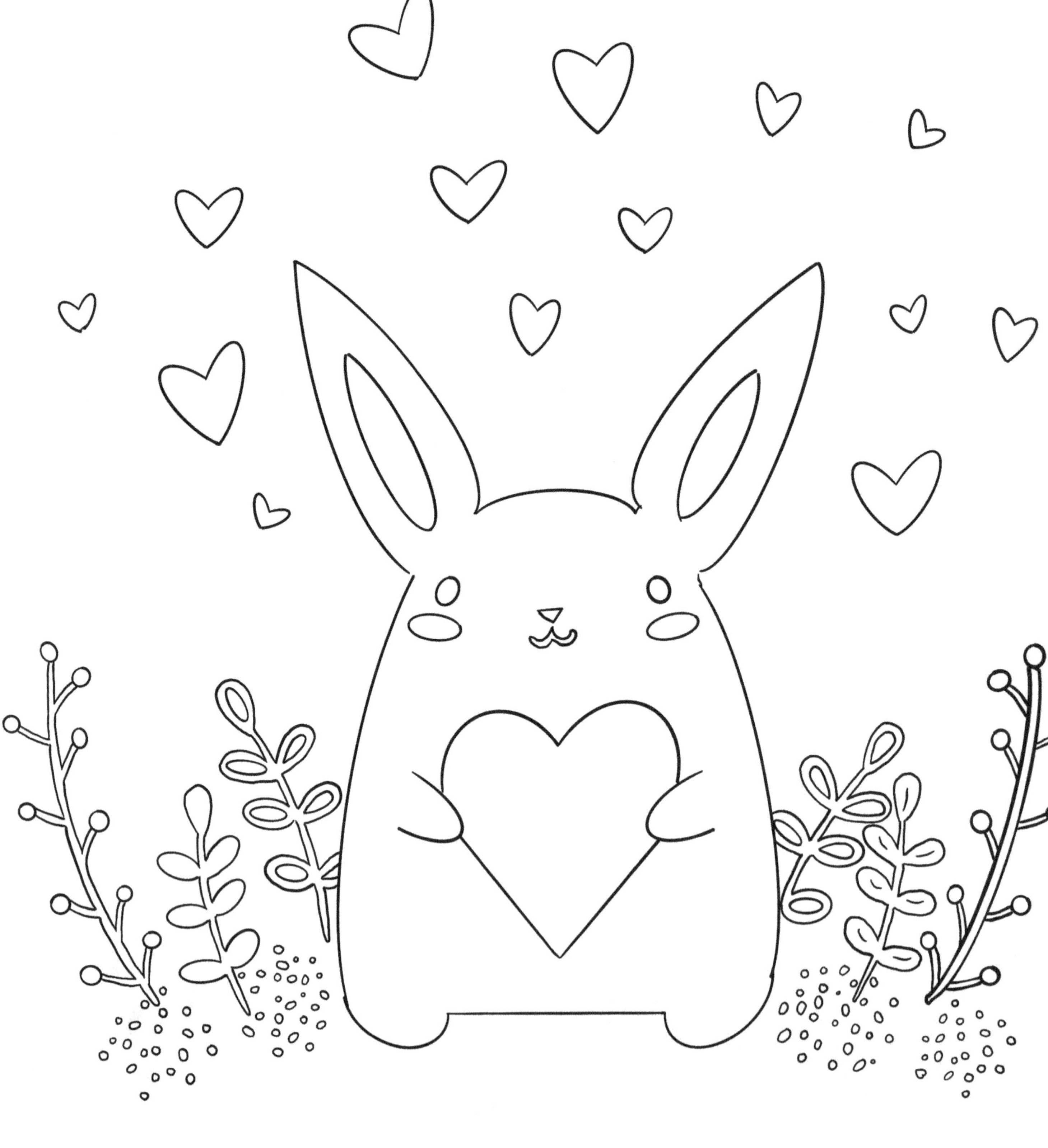

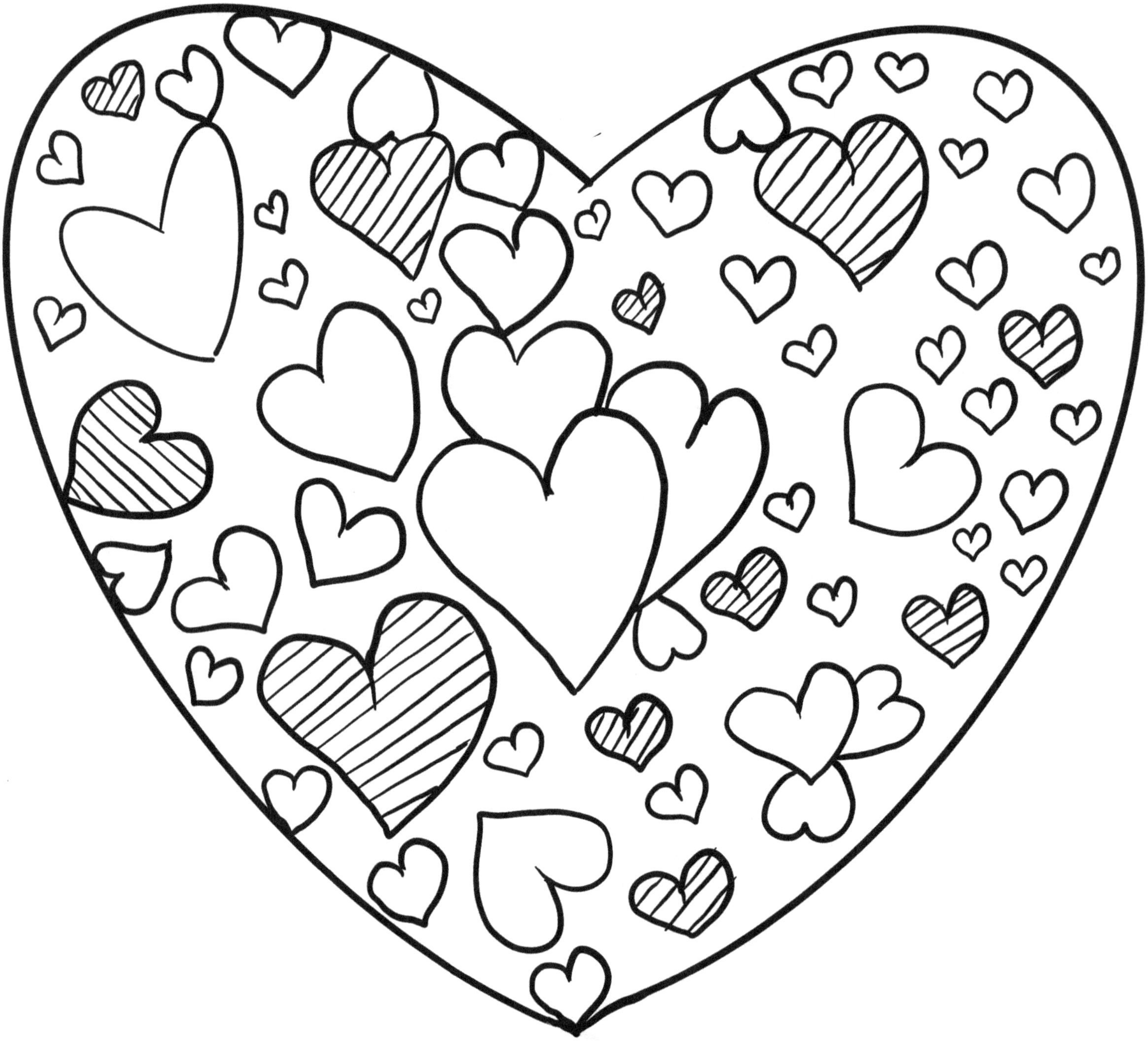

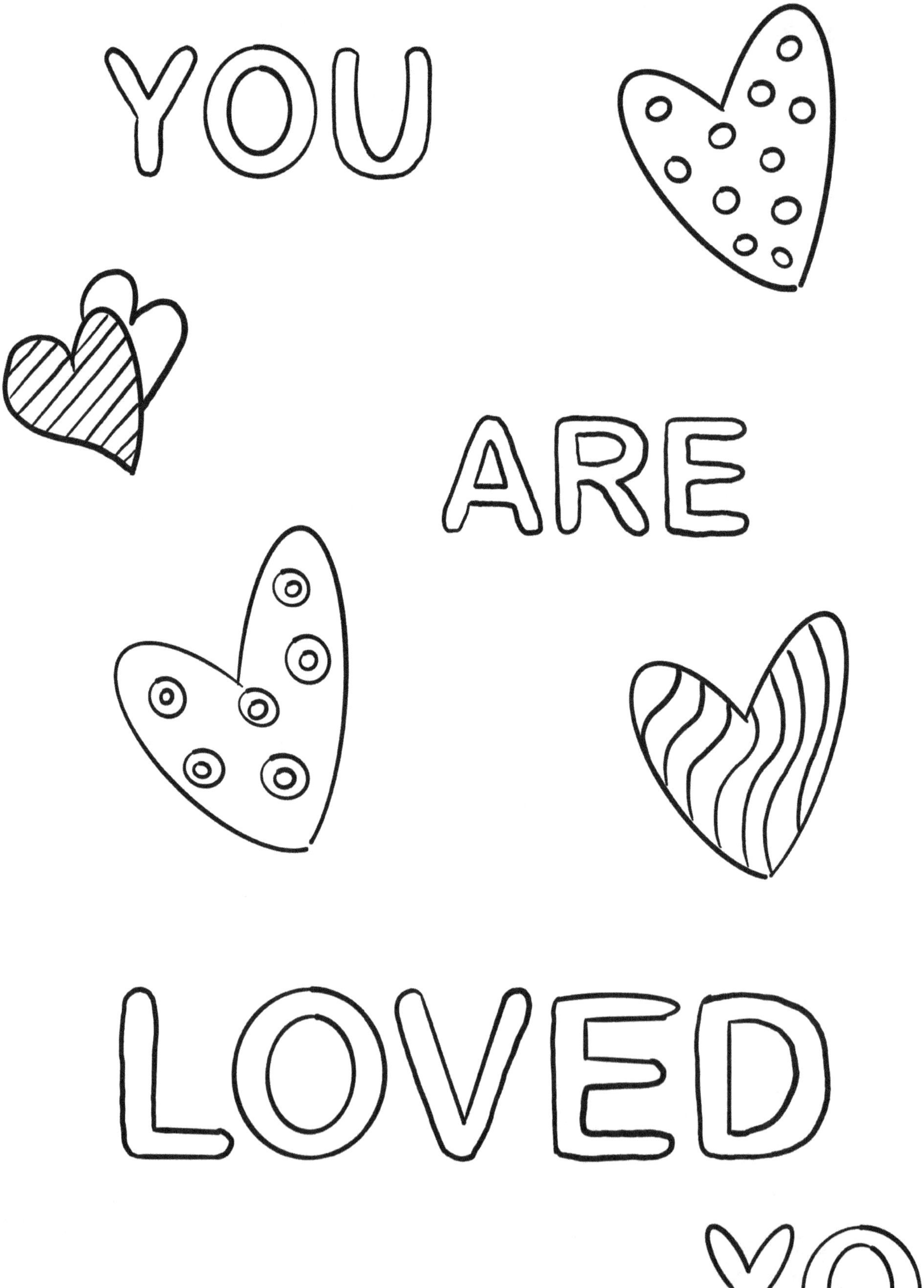
YOU
ARE
LOVED
XO

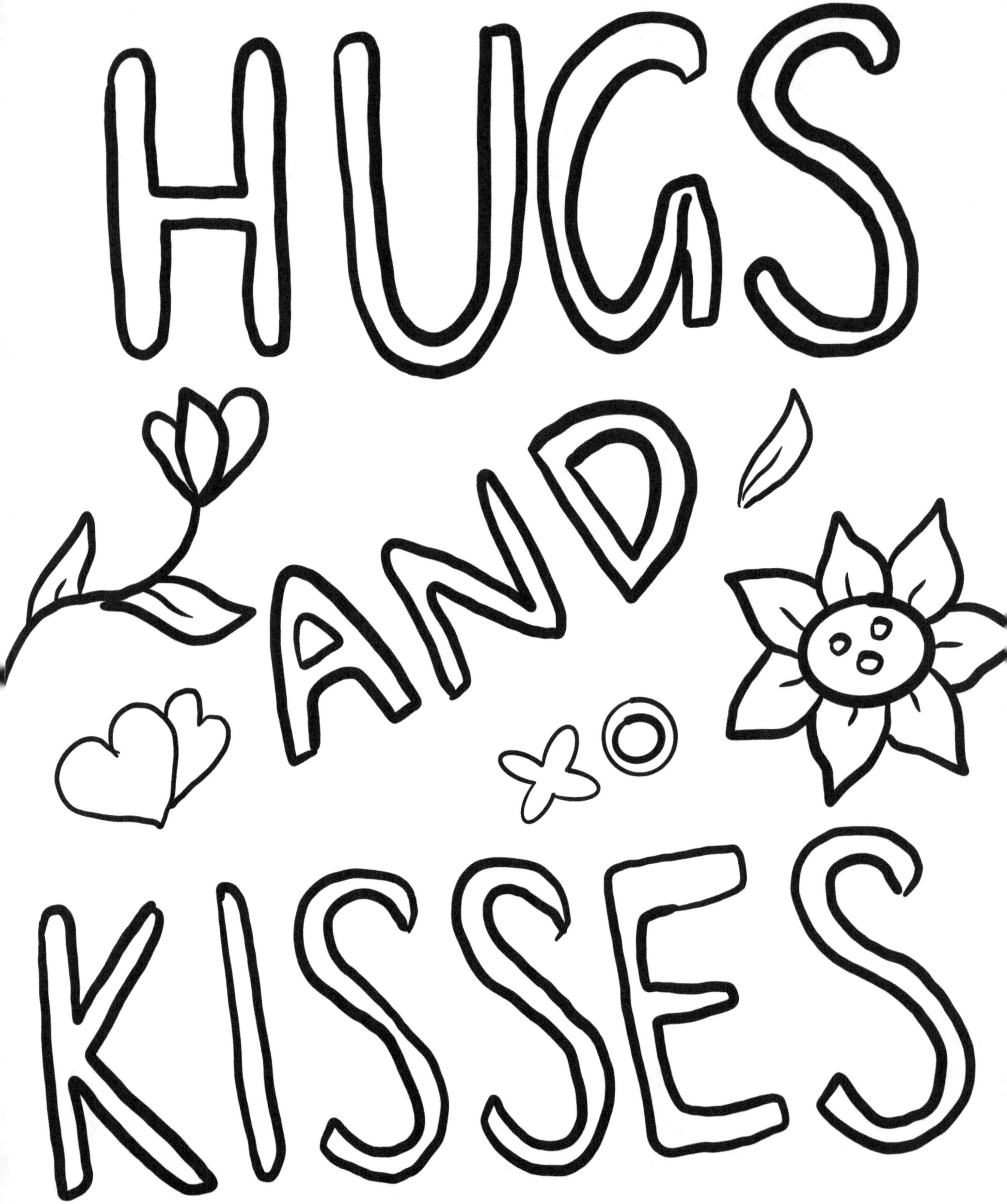
HUGS
AND
XO
KISSES

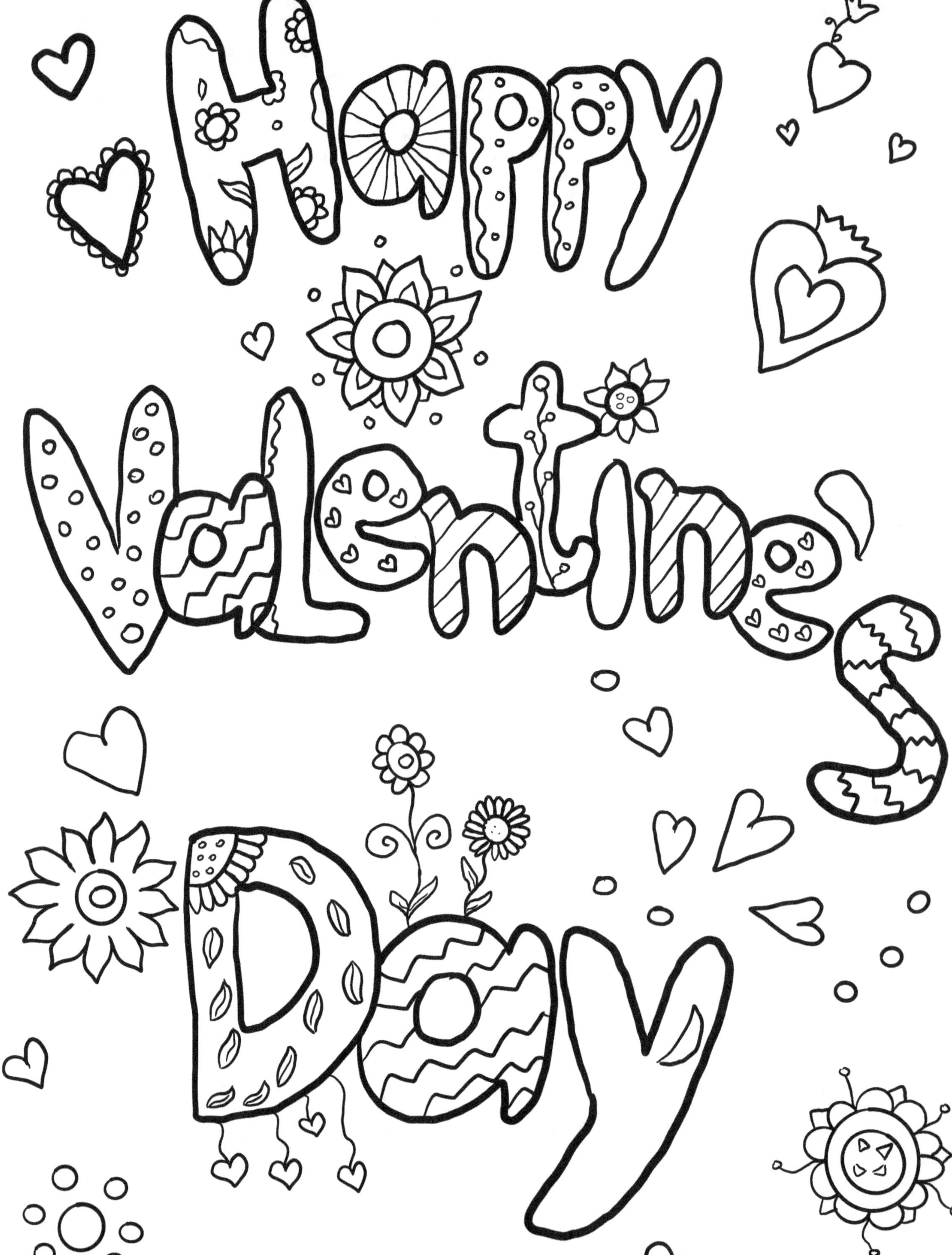
Happy Valentine's Day

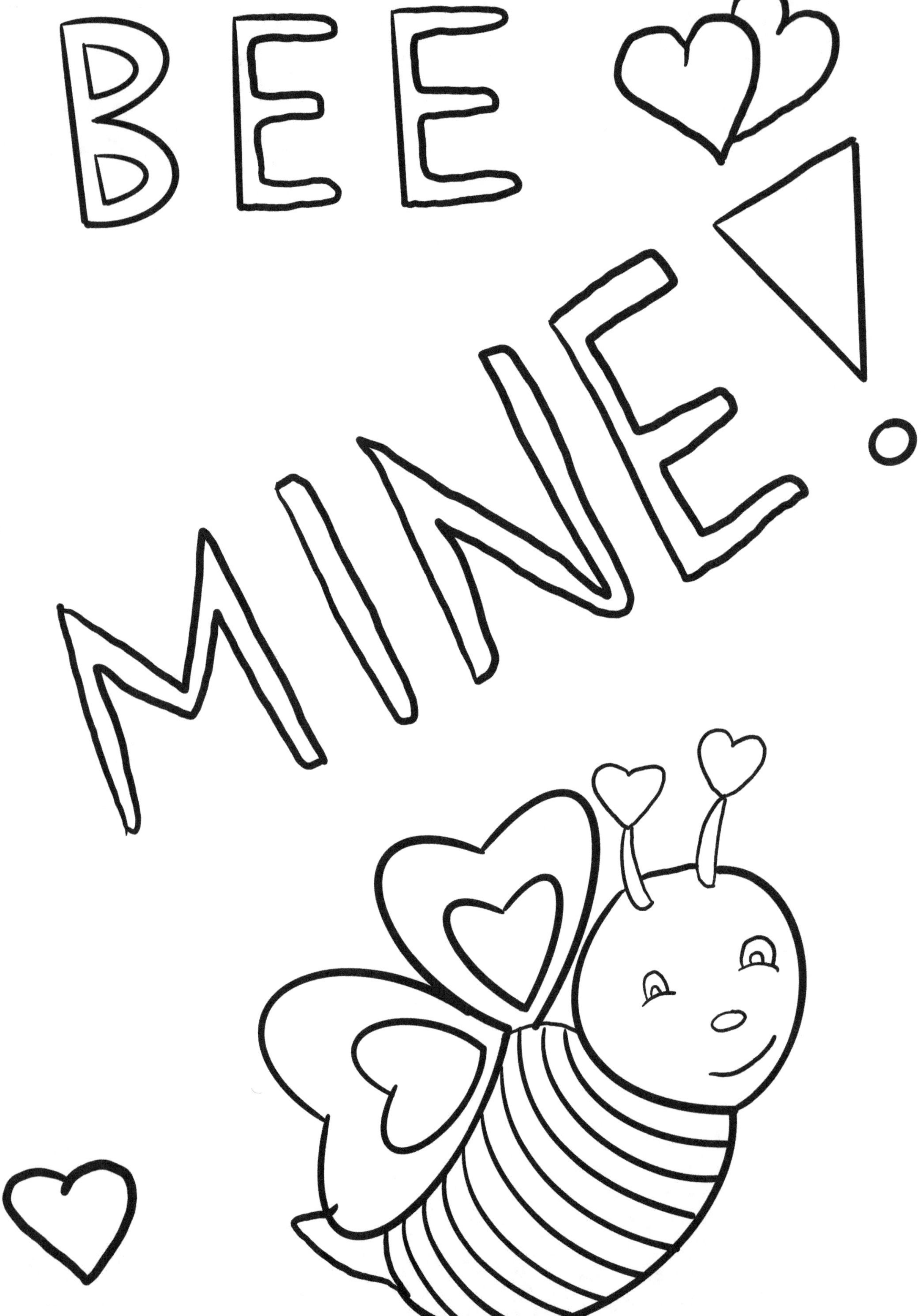
BEE MINE!

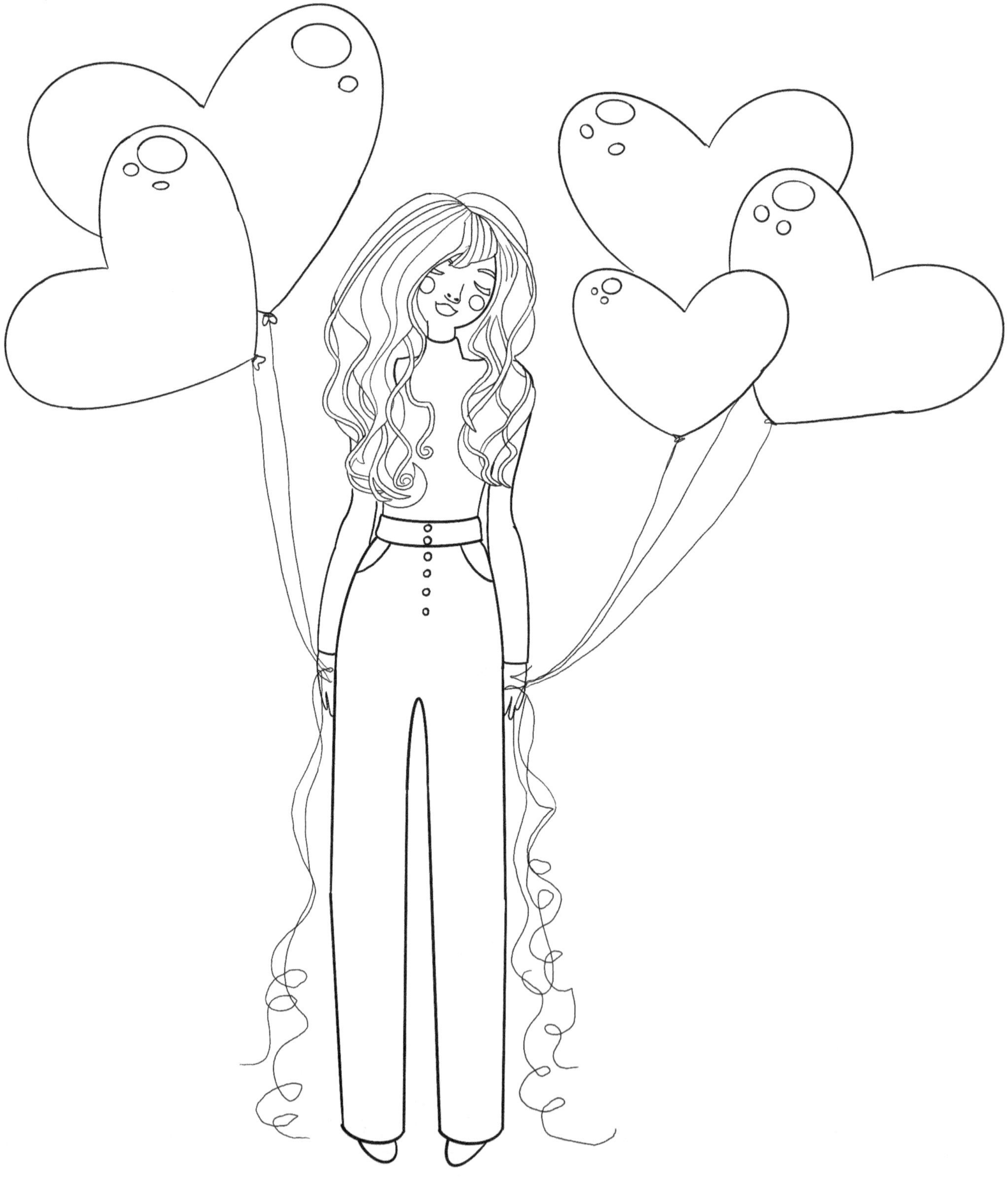

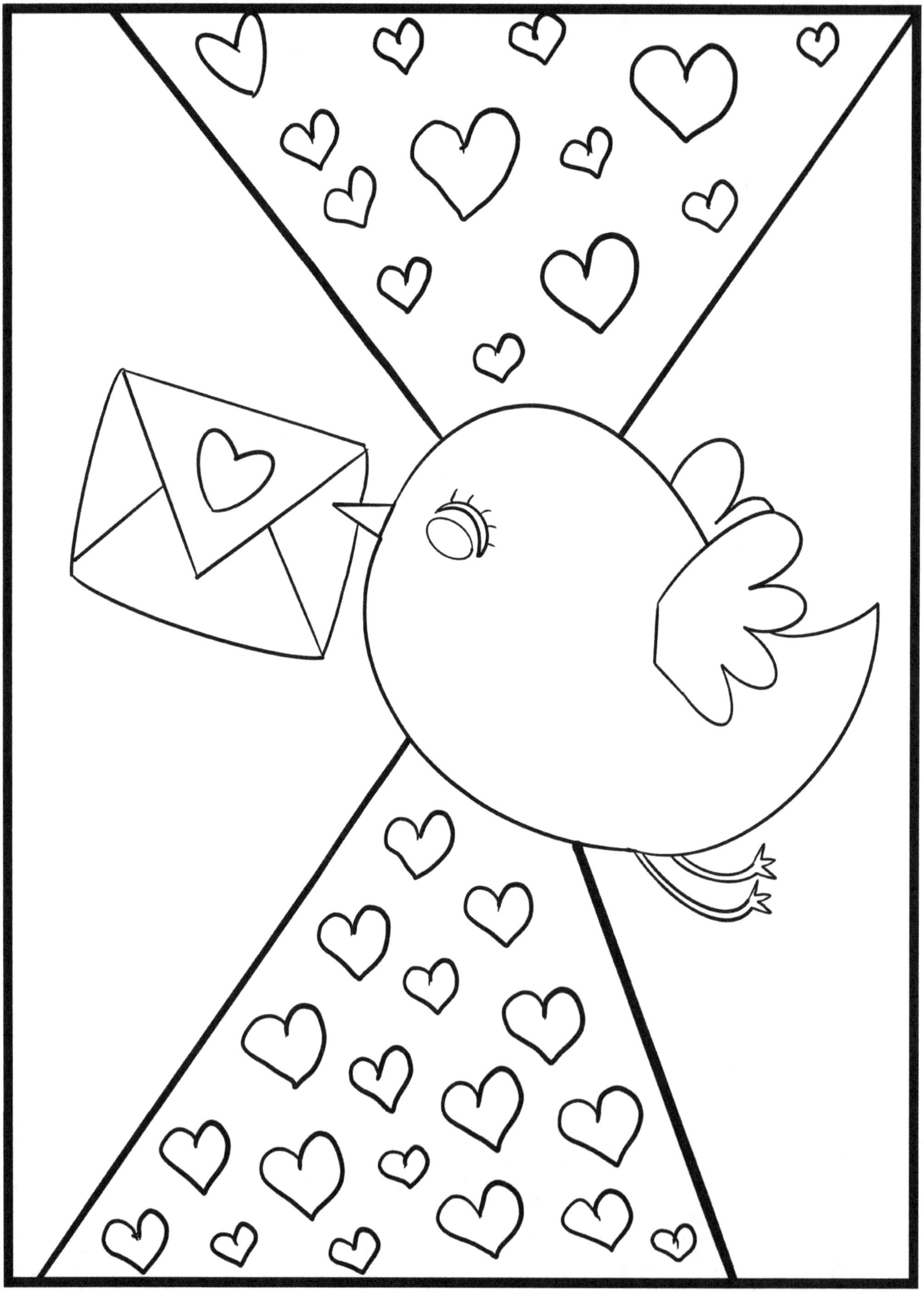

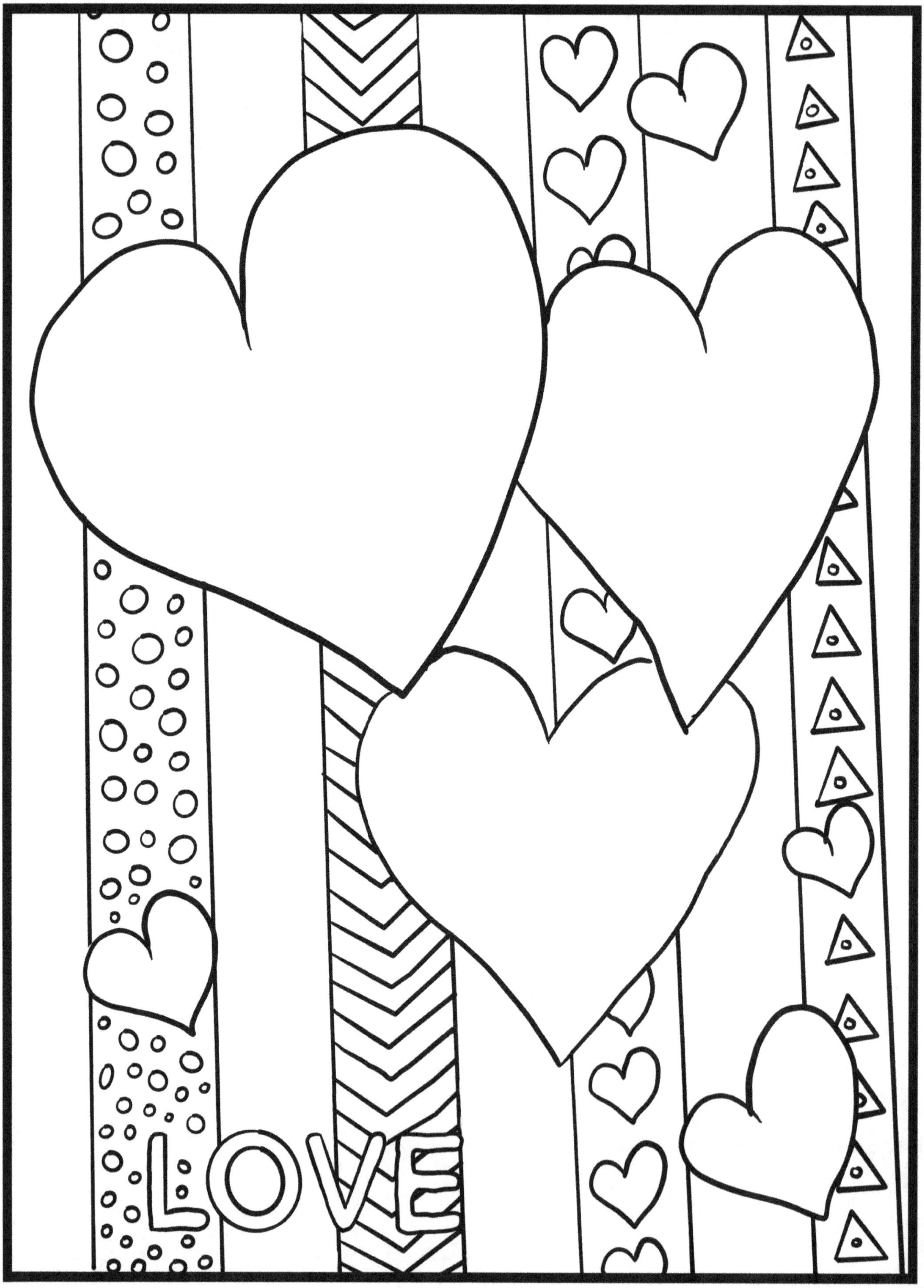
LOVE

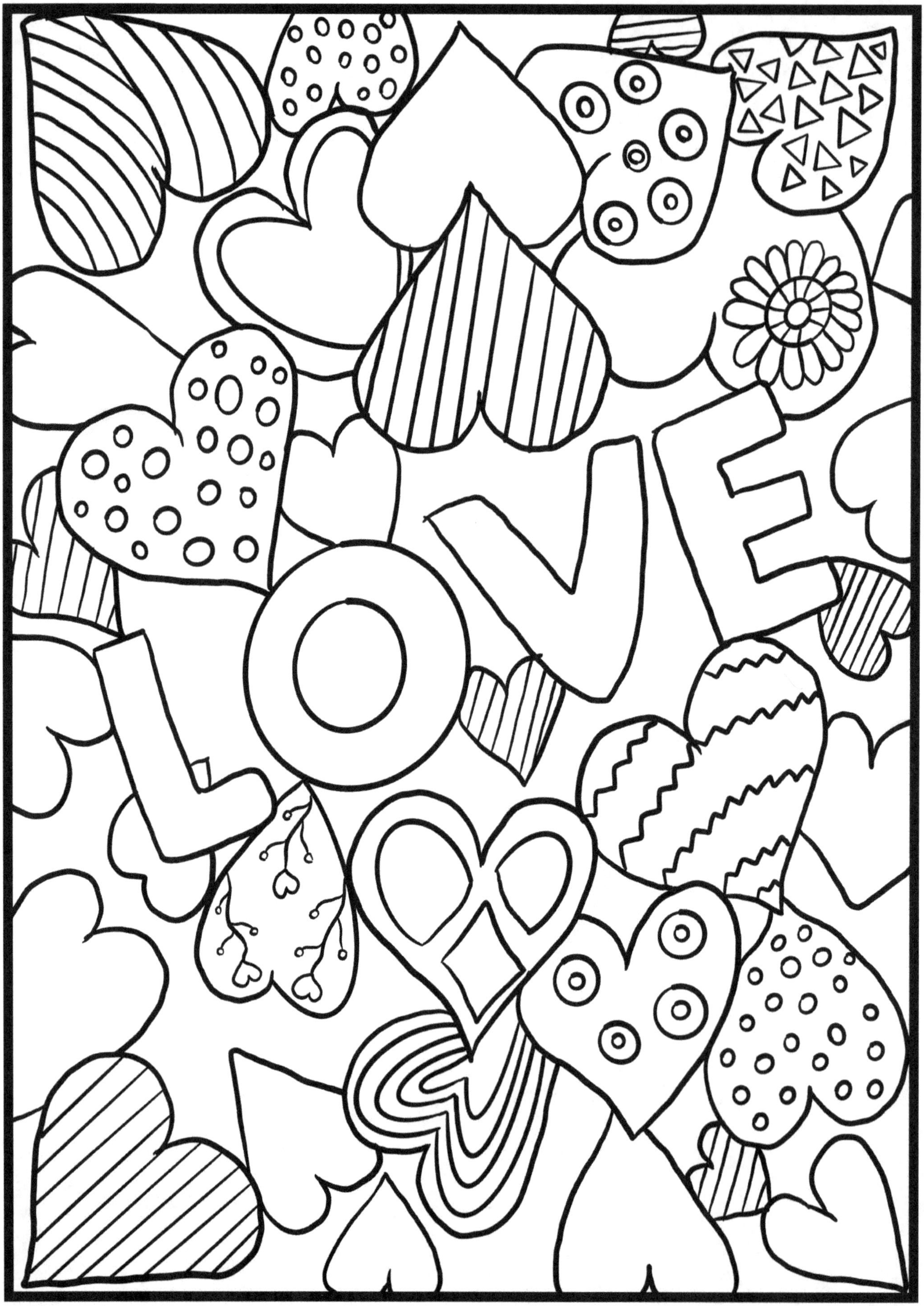
LOVE

www.ingramcontent.com/pod-product-compliance
Lightning Source LLC
Chambersburg PA
CBHW080816220526
45466CB00011BB/3578
* 9 7 8 1 6 5 0 1 8 2 7 1 1 *